T0070278

Love, Sex & Other
THINGS BAD FOR YOU

GARY SOUL

LOVE, SEX & OTHER THINGS BAD FOR YOU

iUniverse books may be ordered through booksellers or by contacting:

iUniverse
1663 Liberty Drive
Bloomington, IN 47403
www.iuniverse.com
844-349-9409

@fromthesoul
@soulwithink
www.soulwithink.com

Illustrations by Dean Martin
@d.gallry

ISBN: 978-1-6632-3726-2 (sc)
ISBN: 978-1-6632-3727-9 (e)

Print information available on the last page.

iUniverse rev. date: 03/31/2022

To anyone who's loved and lost and been brave enough to do it all over again.

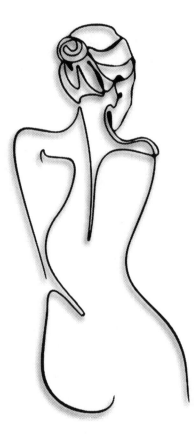

Home

I just want a cup of coffee
and an infinity with You.

I could fill endless pages
with beautiful thoughts of you.

You called me crazy
for falling for You.

Part of me thinks you're 100% right.

Most of me doesn't give a fuck.

We were just idiots addicted to
love, sex and other things
bad for us.

You smiled as you bit my lips
and ran your nails
perfectly down my back.

Last night was a selfish mistake.

We're no better
than a fleeting moment.

Drives that had no destination
with a playlist that never ended.

It was perfect with You.

I want to disappear with You
with nothing more than our
camera and clichés.

A good bottle of wine.
Lo-fi in the background.
Press record.
We loved nights like this.

You stood there
masked in candlelight,
silk barely covering the parts
that I loved to taste.

You pulled me in closer
and my lips met
all the places
you never knew could be kissed.

We could've been more than
heavy hearts and empty promises.

I wish you didn't find your peace
in pieces.

In the same room,
only a few feet away
and we've never been further apart.

Just keep steady
and rest by my side for a moment.
Let me steal away your worries
and remind You that you're golden.

I loved all the shattered pieces
You said were impossible to fix.

We were all the best kinds of crazy.

More black lace.
Less heart breaks.

Fuck it.

Let them watch.

The spontaneous places
turned us on the most.

You begged me to grab your hair
while your wet lips
wrapped around me.

I barely held on.

I lusted for the feel of you
as much as I longed for your
love.

I couldn't tell the difference.

I waited on a ghost.

For now,
find a way to love yourself
before you ask me
to love you again.

"This is goodbye"
I lied so absently.

And I still wonder
what it would've been like
if we stuck through the tough times
and fought for this
just a little bit harder.

Loved a little bit longer.

To me,
you were magic…
impossible to resist.

To you,
I was just an empty bottle of wine
and a night you'll always deny.

I love the way
I leave You breathless
when my tongue and fingers
are swimming in your ocean.

Stuck somewhere between
regret in the morning
and I miss the feel of you.

It was always a toss up
between your smile
and freckles in the sunlight
or your perfect curves
hugged by bedsheets
while you danced
in the moonlight.

I can listen
to your late night whispers forever.

Time stood still
for the most painful memories.

As hard as it was,
I lied and told you
there was nothing left here for you.

For us.

It's better this way.

I've lost count of all the times
I've wanted to call you
in the middle of the night.

I knew better.

Just barely.

Yes, I love you
but I've never needed the bottom
of an empty bottle
to find those words.

Let's lay here and listen
to the rainstorm
while we lie to one another
for a little bit longer.

You promised me forever
and that still wasn't enough time.

My midnight muse.
You're pure magic.

Black lace lingerie polaroids
to fill our red room memories.

I pulled the covers aside
to make sure
you weren't just
a beautiful dream.

You went to war
against your heart
and left me as
the only casualty.

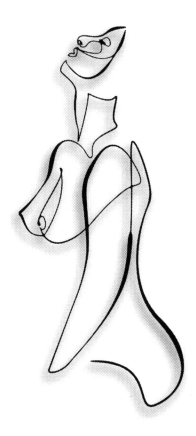

Almost, not really

I'm still haunted by
all of our hopeless maybes.

And even now…
I'm waiting on a fading fantasy.

I'm foolishly patient.

The parts I miss the most
are the things you
barely remember.

You gave me all of your body
but not a single real kiss.
You give me every night
but never a real moment's time.

I want to fulfill
every broken promise
he left you with.

Your kisses told me
everything I needed to know.

Spellbound by your smile.

Falling in love with you
is a beautiful, daily thing.

Sleep soundly tonight
knowing that if your world
ever crumbled, I wouldn't hesitate
to give you mine.

You make it impossible
to get out of bed in the morning
and I love every second of it.

I'll never forget the way
you smiled in Central Park
with snowflakes clinging
onto your fluttering eyelashes.

It was the cruelest game
and neither one of us
could stop playing.

We were all the best things
at exactly the worst times.

Or maybe it was the opposite.

I can't even remember anymore.

I gripped your hips tighter
as you moaned with your face
pressed into the pillow.

I hate to admit that some nights
I miss your voice so much
that I'm willing to
put up with another fight
just to hear it again.

I fell in love with You
surrounded by
clouds of hookah smoke
and a cup of tea
that lasted 'til sunrise.

I fought for a future
with someone who
couldn't let go of her past.

I lost myself
somewhere between
your irresistible lip bites
and empty promises.

Lost words I've wanted to say but
I can't seem to find the right time.
Never the perfect second.
Constantly the wrong minute.
Always a bad hour.

I hate myself
for not being able to hate you.

If you have to go,

go tomorrow.

But for today,

let's pretend everything is okay

and chase another sunrise.

You smiled and in that moment
I knew I would never
stop trying to make
your heart skip beats.

Here.

Now.

We had all the time in the world.

I still get those lingering moments
where I think that you might
come back and I always
try my best to wake myself up
before I fall too deep into
nightmares masked as fairy tales.

I still found a way
to wipe your tears
before I walked away
for the last time.

I promise it'll get better.

Just not with me by your side.

I never knew happiness
could hurt
until I saw you
laughing in his arms.

I hope that you're
happier with him.

I hope that you can tell
I'm lying.

You never needed
a single ounce of fixing.
I'll love You infinitely
just as You are.

You're safe here
tonight and always.

I still blindly entertain
the idea of "us".

All the little notes
that you scribbled in
your favorite book…
Those were the most
beautiful glimpses into
your gorgeous soul.

You stared into the camera
and smiled after you gagged
knowing it drives me crazy.

If that was goodbye
know that I loved You
until the very end.

No.

Even now. Still.
I love You still.

All the ways
You showed me your heart
without saying a single word.

Not lucky enough
to fall asleep with no regrets.

"Yes, please" you begged
as I tightened my hand
around your neck and pressed
deeper into You.

Your eyes locked onto mine
as you tasted yourself off of
the hardest parts of me.

Yours.

Mine.

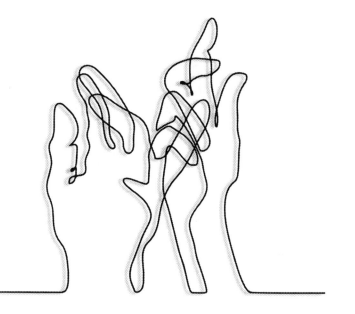

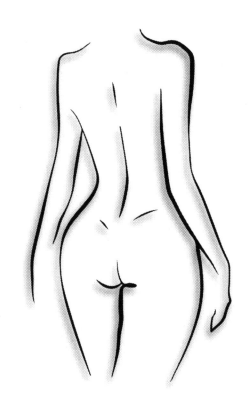

Breathe

@fromthesoul

@soulwithink

<u>www.soulwithink.com</u>

About the Author

Born and raised in Queens, NY, Gary found himself nose deep in books at an early age, eager to consume anything related to sci-fi or fantasy. He attended university on Long Island, graduated with a degree in English Studies and subsequently found himself in the fashion world for over a decade. You can find Gary wandering the city when the weather is warm, searching for the best cup of coffee in NYC and a quaint, plant filled café to people watch in.

Printed in the United States
by Baker & Taylor Publisher Services